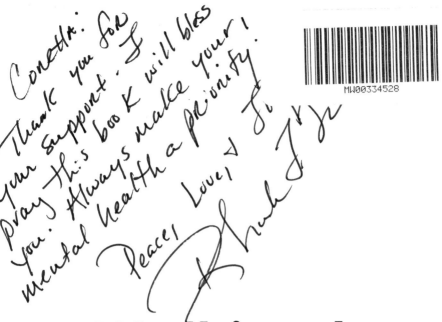

Walking by Faith

Empowering Stories About Women Overcoming Depression

RHONDA FULLER TURNER

Foreword by: Jacqueline F. Houston, Licensed Professional Counselor

Editors: Elaine S. Duke (Senior Editor), Donna D. Lewis, Jacqueline R. Houston, Sharon S. Anderson, Stephanie Andrews

Title: Walking by Faith

Subtitle: Empowering Stories About Women Overcoming Depression

Author: Rhonda Fuller Turner

Published by Celeste Publishing in Richmond, Virginia

First Edition, 2018

Published in the United States of America

Table of Contents

This book is dedicated to all the sistas who suffer in silence with depression. May this book give you a voice and the courage to take control of your mental health.

We overcome by the word of our testimony. (Revelation 12:11)

Acknowledgments

I thank God for giving me the vision and knowledge needed to complete this divine assignment. A special thank you to my Boaz, the Reverend Doctor Michael A. Turner, Sr., for encouraging me to finish what was started over ten years ago and seeing in me what God sees in me. I love you, and I am forever grateful to God for our union. Thank you to my parents, John and Mozelle Fuller, and my little sister, Myra Fuller, for your continued support and encouragement. Thank you to my sista-friends for allowing me to share their stories in my book. Thank you to Dr. Evangelist Lucille Jones and Minister Tiera Owens for your contribution to the book. A special thank you to my friend, Stan Webb, the best graphic designer in the world, who has for over twenty years supported my work. Thank you to Kia Potts and Celeste Publishing for helping to bring the vision to fruition. Thank you to my sista-friends, Sharon Anderson, Stephanie Andrews, Elaine Duke, Donna Lewis, and Jacqueline Houston, for your editorial expertise and friendship. Thank you Paula K. Waller with Thayer Designs for your critique and editorial services. Thank you to Knyla White Harris Photography and CJ Harris Photography for your awesome photography skills. Thank you to Leslie Davis for being the beautiful cover model. Thank you to Darryl Dutch Penick for making my hair and make-up flawless. Thank you to all my other family and friends who gave input and took time to listen to my ideas.

Foreword

And they overcame him by the blood of the Lamb, and by the word of their testimony, and they loved not their lives unto the death. (Revelation 12:11)

It has been my honor to be friends with Rhonda Fuller-Turner for over 25 years. It is a more significant pleasure to provide the foreword for her first of many published works. Rhonda has always been a candid and hard-working person. With that said, it can become startling to have basked in the ongoing life of those to whom you are familiar and not realize the inward struggles until we are faced with the echoing cries of, "Help," from those usually secure places.

As I read *Walking by Faith*, I realized the commonalities of life that we share but not just us but many women we have encountered in life. Rhonda's willingness to present her testimony in a detailed manner encouraged me to examine where my cries for help, turning points, and desire for a personal legacy for others can be shared.

This book gives you testimonies of this process anchored in the acknowledgment to accept what you cannot change on your own and believe in the strength of God to never leave you without a path to hope and wholeness.

Chapter 1

Introduction

A small country church named Watson Level Missionary Baptist Church in Gretna, VA, is where I learned how to "walk by faith and not by sight." I had wonderful role models who shared their testimonies, Sunday after Sunday, of how God had made a way out of no way. I was greatly influenced by the preached Word from Pastors Jack Wilson and the late Katie L. McKenzie. I learned that when one walks by faith out of obedience to God that one can expect to have the victory in any situation. I learned, just as Abraham in Genesis 12:1 experienced, that walking by faith and not by sight requires you to go to a place you do not know, one that God will reveal as you walk in obedience. The journey may seem impossible and crazy at times, but as you continue to trust God and lean on Him for understanding, all that you go through will make sense in the end.

My faith journey began in 1978. I was eight years old, and that was the year I decided to make Jesus my personal Savior. I did not know what I was doing, but I knew that people who received salvation seemed to have a lot to say about how good God had been to them through their many struggles that included financial hardship, job loss, sickness, and death. The testimony seemed to always end with God turning it around and saving them in their moment of distress. I thought to myself, "Wow, if God can do that for them, certainly He can get me through the third grade, and I can learn multiplication." So, I decided to commit myself and my life to the Lord despite the fact that I honestly did not want to go to church. But like many households in the country, it was a requirement. My dad's stern voice would echo on many Sunday mornings when I would wake up dreading the long day at church and attempting to get out of going to church by feigning illnesses, such as sore throats, stomach aches, coughs, and diarrhea. He could see through all my drama and would lay hands on me and say, "You will feel better once you get to church and take it to the altar." On many occasions he reminded me, "When you get a job, pay your bills, and live on your own, you can do whatever you want. Until then, we will serve the Lord, and you will go to church." So with that in mind, I went to church, and I listened to the messages and watched and observed the people in the church very carefully. I never acted out in church because I knew what would happen once I got home. I had a terrible fear of the "black belt" that my father wore around his waist. I knew at any time I could have an intimate encounter with that "black belt." I listened even though, in the beginning, my reasons were selfish that led me to the Lord. I began to grow and learn the traditions of the Black church. I learned that church was the one place where it seemed that no matter what was going on in the home or the community, people felt a peace and freedom to share and lay down their heavy burdens. Everyone left feeling good and uplifted. It was the fuel they needed to get through the week. I began to accept and enjoy going to church every Sunday. My favorite part of the service was the testimony period where it was a real experience to hear people express their faith and belief in God. I enjoyed hearing and seeing how God was moving in the lives of the people in the church.

This leads me to the life-changing memory that I have of the oldest mother in the church. She was a woman of deep faith, and she loved the Lord. She was faithful in her walk with the Lord. Every Sunday she would stand up to testify, and, before giving her testimony, she would say, "I thank God for waking me up, clothed in my right mind!" She would proceed to tell the church how God had been so good to her, how He had provided, made ways out of no way and personally attest to God being her Savior for whatever else had happened that week. She said with a big smile, "I wouldn't take nuthin' for my journey." Now as a child I sat very still in the wooden church pew and tried hard to picture our church mother's mind wrapped up in clothes. It was a visual concept that I just could not grasp. I thought to myself, how could she be thankful if her mind was wrapped in clothes and where were these clothes? I was looking at her and I could not see any signs of clothes wrapped around her head. What a sight that would be if the clothes she wore were wrapped around her head! I remember asking my father once about her statement, and he said, "You will understand it in the by and by." I thought okay, he does not know either and by the way, what is the "by and by?" Certainly, those thoughts never left my mind to become clear questions because of fear that I might have an intimate encounter with the "black belt." He would perceive me as being "sassy" or, as we country people love to say, "being forward."

I continued to observe this church mother, and she became my favorite person to listen to during testimony time in church. Sometimes she would start a song, "We come this far by faith, leaning on the Lord." This song would rally the church, and everyone who sang the hymn seemed to be moved by the words as if it was speaking directly to what they had been through. I remember after her testimony she would break out into a shout and jump around the church praising God until she got exhausted and just laid back on the pew trying to get her breath. I would hear my mother's voice echoing in my mind saying, "It doesn't take all that." At that time, my mother did not believe that people had to shout and jump around the church. She thought they were just performing and, as the old people would say, "They just putting on a show." I thought about what my dad said, and the words of an old spiritual hymn echoed in my ear, "You will understand it better by and by." Now, my mother and I both understand the "by and by" and that it took all that and more. I also understand that God was using this church mother to have a profound impact on my life later.

This church mother had spent her life on a faith journey with God. She had raised her children and she was also helping to raise her grandchildren at the time. Through her testimony, I knew that she had been through some storms and struggles in her life and knew how to praise God in and out of the storms. She had been through troubled times that required her to spend time on her knees praying, knowing this was how to get a prayer through. I don't know this to be true, but I believe there were times when this church mother felt like giving up and losing her mind. After all, if she did not have these thoughts, she would not have been thanking God for keeping her in her right mind. My spiritual imagination believes if I could talk to her right now she would say, "I had some good days and I had some bad days. I had some days where I felt like I would lose my mind but I won't complain because God brought me through clothed and in my right mind."

She went home to be with the Lord years ago, but her spirit still lives on. As I move forward in life, I look back on those days at Watson Level Baptist Church and thank God for my space in the building. I thank God for using this church mother to touch me in such a spiritual way. Later in life, I would draw strength from this church mother's testimony and the Word of God. I would come to realize that my faith journey would take me many places and there would be some obstacles along the way, but my faith and trust in God would help me to endure and continue walking by faith.

Let me take you on my journey and the journey of other Black women and how we connected with our faith and mental health. If there was ever a time that Black women needed confirmation and validation to seek professional help and still have a relationship with God...the time is now. More single moms are performing dual roles in raising families that have absentee fathers. The stressors of day-to-day life and the financial responsibilities are significant. The pressures of exceeding society's expectations weigh heavily on us, and we strive to keep up, but sometimes we fall.

Throughout history, it is the Black woman who has had to shoulder the responsibility of being the one to keep the family together and stay strong. In slavery, when the men were separated and torn from their families, it has been the women left to carry on. Back then, women had no time to crumble; they had to endure and go on. So we have gone on for generations since slavery, continuing to take care of everyone else and forgetting to take care of ourselves. Modern-day slavery is when our men have been torn away to prisons, drugs, and the streets. Some Black women have been experiencing breakdowns for years because of the demands of taking care of and providing for their families. They have become experts at masking their true emotions in public. We don't see the women who cry themselves to sleep in fetal positions or cry out to God for help. We don't look at the women who contemplate suicide because things have gotten so bad and they don't want to go on. We don't see the women who see their children and want to take the very life they birthed. We don't look at the women who are caught up in the grips of addiction and, with each hit of the pipe, secretly wish that they would do enough to end the nightmare. We don't see the women, who have loved hard and have given their all to who they thought was Mr. Right, only to find out that he is Mr. Wrong. Finally, we don't see the women who find themselves homeless and unable to feed their children.

In Black culture, it has been taboo to talk about mental illness. I can remember my grandmother saying, "What goes on at home stays at home. Don't be airing your family's dirty laundry and don't tell them white folks anything." Growing up, I remember very few people who had a mental illness. It was viewed as a sign of weakness and they were looked down upon. I remember one woman who had committed a heinous crime and she was found not guilty because of insanity. She spent a few months in the psychiatric hospital and when she returned home, we were told not to go near her or we would be crazy too. Now that I look back, she had suffered years of depression and abuse at the hands of her abusive husband. She snapped and went into survival mode. She could not take it anymore and violently killed her husband. Her family did not support her, and she was left to deal with her issues in isolation.

The Black experience dealing with mental illness has not been positive. Mental illness has been around a long time and has had a profound impact on the Black culture. Am I saying that Black women are crazy? No, I am saying that according to the Diagnostic Manual of Statistics, depression is a mental illness, and I believe it's time to call "a spade a spade." I think the time is now to take a stand and let people know that it can get better, but we must first admit that there is a problem. The time is now to stop the insanity of denial. What is the definition of insanity? It is doing the same thing and expecting different results. Let's do something new and get results! Let's talk about the taboo subject of mental illness and be supportive of women who are dealing with depression and other mental health issues.

Let's put a face to mental illness. As a young, educated, and intelligent Black woman, I found myself needing the very mental health system that had become my livelihood. One might say, how does that happen? It happens when you repress your feelings and you think you have it all under control. Then you find that your life is spinning out of control. Here is where my journey begins and the passage of other strong Black women who have found themselves asking these questions:

Why can't I get out of bed?

Why can't I stop crying?

I gave birth to this baby, but I don't love this baby?

What's happening to me?

Who is this person who has taken over my life?

Where is God? Why doesn't He take it away?

Do I seek help? Where do I go?

What will my friends and family think if I start taking medications?

Am I really "crazy?"

Chapter 2

Depression in Black Women

According to the DSM-5, a manual used to diagnose mental disorders, depression occurs when you have at least five of the following symptoms at the same time:

- *A depressed mood during most of the day, particularly in the morning*
- *Fatigue or loss of energy almost every day*
- *Feelings of worthlessness or guilt almost every day*
- *Impaired concentration, indecisiveness*
- *Insomnia (an inability to sleep) or hypersomnia (excessive sleeping) almost every day*

- *Markedly diminished interest or pleasure in nearly all activities nearly every day*
- *Recurring thoughts of death or suicide (not just fearing death)*
- *A sense of restlessness or being slowed down*
- *Significant weight loss or weight gain*

Research shows that there are higher rates of depression among African American women and low rates of treatment. This is not a surprising find when one considers our culture and our history of women taking care of everyone else before their own needs. Many of us grew up in homes where it is regarded as a sign of weakness for a woman to seek mental health treatment. Our society does not equate mental health and physical health the same. In fact, there is a stigma when one says they are "mentally ill." Often this statement is followed by strange looks and separation from the person as if they have a plague that can be transmitted from being in one's presence. When you tell someone that you have been diagnosed with a physical illness like cancer, one immediately receives a more compassionate response such as, "What can I do to help you?" This has not always been the case, however. In the beginning, cancer was a stigmatizing disease as well. However, with education, advocacy, and people sharing their personal stories, it changed the way our world viewed this disease. The hope for mental illness is that one day people will be able to share openly. Today, the myth is Black women don't get depressed. The reality is we do get depressed and many women go to jail and/or their graves with undiagnosed and untreated depression. It's unfortunate when we see Black women killing their babies and themselves because they suffer from undiagnosed depression.

Family members miss the signs of depression because we have not taken time to educate ourselves on the issue of mental illness. We lose the signs when we see family members going through difficulty because we think that it only affects white women, and we believe we are "stronger than that." I hope that as a result of reading this book that you will know the signs and symptoms of depression and be able to help friends and family members who may be struggling with depression. I desire that you will start the conversation with someone else and educate others to become a part of the solution and take the stigma away from mental illness.

Chapter 3

A Black Woman's Struggle with Depression

"Many are the afflictions of the righteous: but the LORD delivereth him out of them all" (Psalm 34:19).

Who am I? I am a 35-year-old (at the time I first started writing this book) divorced Black woman who loves the Lord with all her heart and soul. I work for a public health agency in the capacity of Program Manager. I work with mental health, substance abuse, and HIV-diagnosed clients. I have a Master's in Addiction Counseling. I am state and nationally certified as an addiction counselor. I have worked in this field for 12 years. I am a member of Alpha Kappa Alpha Sorority, Incorporated and The Links, Incorporated. I have received numerous awards and recognition for outstanding public service. I sit on various boards in the Lynchburg community. I have been named as one of Lynchburg's Emerging Leaders and have had several published articles. I am the Co-founder of the Coalition for HIV Awareness and Prevention of Central Virginia, Incorporated. I have owned and operated my own business. I could go on, but the goal is not to boast about what I have accomplished, but to set the stage and dispel the myths of the stereotypes about people who have a mental illness.

I grew up in a small town with both parents present in the household. I have one sister. My sister and I always knew that we were loved and had everything we needed. We had problems, but my parents stayed together, and they have been married for 48 years and counting. What a blessing because there were times that I thought they would be a statistic for divorce, but they hung in there and made it work. Today, they are inseparable. It looks as if they have fallen in love all over again. I had their love and support throughout my formative and college years. There were times in my life that I experienced periods of sadness and loneliness. These moments did not last long, but I can remember being around eight years old after I accepted the Lord as my Savior when I first had feelings of heaviness and sadness. I found it hard to concentrate on school and work. I would often think of death and how I would die. I was not suicidal and did not have a plan, but I often wondered if I might be better off dead. Again, to the person on the outside looking in, life was grand because I had loving parents and friends, and I was very active in school. When my mind took me to those thoughts of death, I would pray and ask God to remove them and there would be peace. I was eight years old when I heard the Lord say to me that I would do excellent work for Him and that He would be with me wherever I go. I would go through some painful periods, but He would be with me. The periods of sadness would continue on and off into adulthood. I would keep silent and not even breathe a word about it to anyone for fear that they would think that I was "crazy." I often wondered if any of my friends had the same bouts of sadness, but I dared not ask anyone, not even my best friend. I pushed through those times in silence.

The dark, cold winter season in my life started two years after I got married. This season taught me many lessons but also revealed the source of my sadness. I married a hard-working, educated man who was not to be compared to the other men I had dated in my life. I met him around the time I was having one of my periods of sadness. When we met, I thought to myself, "What a wonderfully sweet guy...my knight in shining armor." Everything was perfect and I was happy. No periods of sadness, just happiness during our courtship. I believed that God had answered my prayers of sending a good man. He was not active in a local church, but he said he believed in God. I rationalized that he was a good man and I was a spiritually rooted woman who would role model and lead him to the Lord. After all, I believed the Lord had sent him my way. I had been through too many relationships with "bad boys" that left me emotionally unstable. When my knight in shining armor rode into my life, I knew that life had to get better.

Now, spiritually grounded Ms. Perfect was not without her issues from life. Again, I had struggled with periods of sadness since I was eight years old. I had my problems with past hurts that I had repressed. Jumping from one bad relationship to another and never taking time to discover who I was were indications that I needed time to work on my issues of self-worth and self-acceptance. I threw myself into my work and other community activities, anything to avoid looking at my problems and to avoid the feelings of sadness. I worked three jobs and took care of everybody except for me. I was too busy working on my career, going to school, and actively working in the women's ministry at church. Who had time for me? I was so busy working and doing everything else that I did not see my marriage headed for a major collision. I remember my dad saying, "Baby, I know you are a hard worker and want things in life, but you need to spend more time at home." My response was, "Daddy, you don't understand, this works for us (meaning my husband and me), and we get along well because when we see each other, we don't have time to fuss or fight. We treasure our time together." Who was I kidding and what planet was I living on? Certainly, not earth.

About two years after our marriage, the whole dynamic of our marriage changed. My husband stopped spending time with me, and he was working all the time. I started to feel like something was wrong and that I needed to be at home cooking and making sure that the house was clean. I had not been a good housekeeper because I was working all the time. This was so ironic because at the same time I was thinking about quitting my jobs, Vanessa, my prayer partner and my good friend, said, "The Lord told me to tell you to go home." I decided to quit all my part-time jobs and just work my full-time job. In my mind, this would make everything better. I would be at home, and, when my husband came home, dinner would be ready, the clothes would be washed, and I would be waiting. What fairy tale was I living in? This was the beginning of the nightmare.

I was coming home and keeping my house clean and preparing meals and my husband would not even notice that the house was clean. He would not even eat the meals prepared because he would get home so late. The sadness began to creep back in, and it came back stronger this time. I was very emotional and I would cry almost every night. I was still attending church and believing God to fix my husband and get him on the same level spiritually that I was. I felt good when I was in church, but then when I came home, I was dealing with the sadness. I was not able to recognize the signs at first, but I was showing symptoms of depression. Now, isn't that something, working in the mental health field, working with clients who were depressed, and I could not see those same symptoms in myself? I was eating everything in sight and my hips were growing every day. Food was my comfort and I gained 50 pounds to prove it. At this time, I also picked up another habit—spending money. I started shopping and buying everything in sight at my husband's expense. I charged any and everything. If someone needed something, I would buy it for them. I charged things to his credit that were ridiculous. I would say to myself, "Well, he should be here with me, so I will teach him to leave me at home. In my mind, I rationalized that I deserved everything that I would buy, which compounded our problems. I was putting us in debt all because I was lonely and depressed.

At that time, I was not feeling good about myself. I was overweight and my relationship with my husband was deteriorating. I had all of my friends praying for God to save my husband, but, it seemed like the more I prayed, the worse it was getting. The tension between my husband and I was getting thick. I began to question him on his work hours, and he became defensive and stayed away from home even more. I had been taught to turn it over to God and He will fix everything, so I screamed out to Him, "Help Me...I don't want to be a divorce statistic." I would fast and pray. I believed God would help me. However, when I came off the fast, nothing had taken place except for losing 10-15 pounds, only to gain it back in two weeks because I was so depressed that the situation had not changed but appeared to be worse.

God revealed to me that my husband was having an affair, and if that was not bad enough, it was with a woman I knew. Even worse, this affair had been going on for quite some time. He denied it even when I had proof that he was involved with this woman. I started to think, "How had this happened? Was I not good enough? Why did my marriage have to suffer? How could I fix it?" I wanted it repaired right away but what I soon learned is that I had no control over the situation. I was in a deep black hole of despair, and I felt like I could not get out and that no one could reach me. I could not even hear from God. He was quiet.

So how did my life look? What did I feel like? I could not sleep, and the food was the one thing that made me feel good. I felt full when I ate, and when I did not eat, I felt empty. My mind and thoughts were consumed with thoughts of my husband with another woman. I would drive around at night with no destination in mind and think how easy it would be to steer into something... anything to stop the emotional torment. Yes, at this time, I was suicidal, but I did not want to kill myself. I just wanted to stop hurting! One might also say I was even homicidal because my husband would come home after spending all night out and want to spend time with me. I would want to take something and end his life, but I would give in to his demands because I wanted it to be like it used to be after a night of passion. I would end up feeling worse than I felt before.

Inside I knew that it was over, but because I had made a vow, I kept wanting to fix it and make it right. I was struggling mentally, physically, and spiritually with doing the right thing. I knew that he would never divorce me, but I could not go on like this. I told him that he needed to get out. I was on an emotional roller coaster. My state of mind now changed to feeling like a failure that my marriage had not worked and I had displeased God. Why did I get married? Was it to avoid feeling lonely and sad? Was it for financial security? Was it because I felt like this was a good time to be married and add this to my résumé?

I struggled with these questions to the point that when he finally moved out, I had my breaking point. I ran the gamut of emotions which led me to uncontrollable crying, inability to focus, loss of appetite, and loss of interest in things that I had once enjoyed. I hit rock bottom, and I remember forcing myself out of bed to go to work and getting there finding myself locked behind my office door not able to move and crying out to God, "Please help me. "Where are You! I need You! I can't do this without You!" And as I sat in my office crying uncontrollably, I picked up the phone without hesitation and called a friend and I remember saying, "Pick me up and take me to the doctor, I need help. I can't stop crying; I can't get it together." She picked me up. I went to the doctor, and he gave me an anti-depressant, and I felt for the first time what my clients feel when they come into my office for help. I felt vulnerable.

It was my aha moment. I was walking in their shoes when I realized that I was no different from my clients, and I began to see our commonalities. Yes, I understood it from the other side of the desk. Their fears had become my fears, their concerns had become my concerns, and their struggles had become my struggles. As I sat waiting to receive instructions and direction on how to move on with my life, I listened to the doctor as he told me how to take the medication prescribed for me and what I might expect. As I sat there, I heard the voices of my past, my grandmother the strong matriarch, saying, "Don't tell those white people your business." I was confused for a moment because I am educated and I know better, but her voice is still echoing, and I have conflicting thoughts of how disappointed she would be in me and the idea that maybe she is right. Perhaps I can get through this without medication. I even thought I would be helpful and polite and accept the drugs but not have to take them. Then I said, "Who am I kidding? I need this, and if grandma had been educated and informed about mental illness, she probably would have taken it too."

The first pill to take was hard for me, but as I moved into acceptance, I did what I needed to do for my mental health and took my medication as directed. I dreaded telling my parents because I knew they would not understand. I did not want them to think I was crazy. My parents' solution was to pray and move on, but it was not that simple. I had been praying, and I had been praying since I was eight years old, and I had been dealing with this. My marriage did not cause this; it just triggered what I had been avoiding most of my life. They were supportive, but I think I was the guinea pig of the family because no one had ever verbalized they were taking medication for their mind. They watched me as I continued to take the medication. I would tell them on a regular basis how I felt, and I shared with them that I thought the medication was working. I had been on the medication for some months when one day my mother said, "Rhonda, you are back to your old self because I can see you smiling and your eyes have hope." I did not know that my eyes were looking so hopeless and I was looking that bad, so it was a surprise when she made that statement. I told her that I felt much better, but I was weaning myself off the medication with the help of my doctor because I did not feel I needed it. She paused and said, "Are you sure?" I thought she would have been jumping for joy, but I guess she had watched the process of me going from being severely depressed and down to living and enjoying life again.

God showed me that He had used me in my family to dispel myths of the type of people who take medication and that medications can improve your life and not make you worse. I was spiritually, physically, and mentally broken when I sought help, and I know that it was a combination of prayer, medication, and family/friend support that helped me to put the broken pieces of my life back together.

Chapter 4

Why Talk About It Now?

Today, I am audacious enough to tell the story of my pain and struggles with depression. Why now? I could have taken my struggle with me to my grave and never breathed a word. The time is now because I know someone else out there may be struggling with depression or other mental health issues and afraid to seek help. If one woman will connect with my story or the other stories and seek assistance as a result of reading this book, then this book will have served its purpose. If as a result of what you read, you can help family members and friends get help, this book will have been worth it. I am putting my face and name out there as a person who struggled with depression who can enjoy recovery because of the God I serve and supportive family and friends in my life. I believe that there was a purpose in my pain and I was put here to be an encourager and to show others the way. Deliverance did not come from running around the church seven times and being delivered instantly. I am not saying that some people cannot be immediately healed because I believe they can, but that was not my journey. I can tell you that without prayer and understanding in the supernatural powers of God to restore my sanity, I might still be at a loss.

I believe that God gifted the psychiatrist to be able to provide services. I also think that God allowed medications to be created for our use. I know that everything that God let me go through was for my testimony and to help others. I hope that churches would become sensitive to mental health issues and encourage people to pray, get counseling, and, if needed, take medication. Medication is not the answer for everyone, but unless you are a professional mental health provider, you cannot discourage people if they need it. If a person was diagnosed with hypertension or diabetes, would you encourage him or her not to take his/her medications? Our society must remove the stigma of mental health and become sensitive to people who struggle in this area. I believe the most significant help to people with mental health issues is having a support system and someone they can talk to. I was very fortunate that

I had my family, good friends, and people who were licensed, professional counselors. Therapy works and everyone should experience seeing a therapist just for the experience even if you think that you have no problem. The experience is a gift to yourself.

God took a very dark and stormy time in my life and turned it into something beautiful. He took away the shame, guilt, and anger associated with that time. My misery turned it into my ministry. As I look back over my life, it is no coincidence that I began to struggle with depression at the same time I accepted Jesus as my personal Savior. The devil wanted to take me out because he knew God had a great plan for my life. What the devil meant for harm, God turned it around for my good. He gave me a testimony to share with the world and to help other women who find themselves struggling with depression.

I have given you a glimpse of just one season of my life and I pray that my transparency will encourage others as they seek to connect with their faith and mental health. Many will judge me after reading my story, and some will analyze it and say that I just needed Jesus. They would be right because I did need Jesus, and I believe that He was there with me the whole time. He was there with me when I met Him at eight years old. He was there through every bout of sadness and depression. He was there the day I picked up the phone and called my friend. He was there in the doctor's office. He was even there when I was taking medications. Jesus was there with me when no one else was there. He is with me now as I am experiencing the freedom of deliverance and recovery. I once thought that what I was feeling was unique to me until I began to share and talk to other black women who had struggled with depression as well. The next chapters of this book are dedicated to highlighting other black women's stories and their struggle. We are not unique and we are not alone. We are overcomers because of our faith and our belief. We went through our battle with depression to help other women who may be experiencing feelings of hopelessness and despair. We have become a light and a testament to how God can keep you if you walk by faith.

Chapter 5

Lucille's Struggle with Depression
(77 years old)

Depression is defined as a mental disorder marked by sadness, inactivity, difficulty in thinking and concentration, and feelings of sorrow. I will add mental anguish with these. Sad to say, this is a condition that afflicts many people, both male and female from all over the world. It transcends racial and economic status. It attacks the homeless living on the streets and the princess living in the palace.

I am a middle-class female who is well-educated and loves the Lord. However, I have had my bouts of severe depression. Looking back on my childhood, it was filled with periods of depression. I lived in a constant state of sadness, which I now recognize as ongoing periods of depression. For me, my depression was brought on by the horrific occurrences during childhood which carried over into my adult years. As a child, I created for myself space where I could go within myself and life would be beautiful. This was how I coped with depression as a child.

At about eight years of age, I had an event happen to me that was hard for a little girl like me to handle. Some older girls were chasing me, and I ran out into the street, right into the side of a moving radio cab. The impact knocked me all the way back to the curb and into a light pole. Somehow I stayed on my feet. I wasn't seriously hurt. The police came and said I was alright and sent me home. The same girls who were chasing me helped me and my little brother get to my house. I now know they weren't going to do anything to me. They just wanted to scare me and have a little bit of what they would call fun at my expense. Well, they did an excellent job.

In my way of thinking, everyone else had done bad things to me and they would be no different. My left knee was injured; I could hardly walk on it and it hurt so badly. When I got to my house, I got in our little bed and just laid there feeling numb. My brother and I had not eaten the entire day, but I didn't feel hungry anymore. I remember that awful pain in my knee got worse whenever I tried to get my leg in a more comfortable position. Even though the pain was excruciating, I just couldn't bring myself to shed a tear.

As I lay in bed that night, I was looking into the sky. I remember lying there, but I didn't know where I was or even who I was. I remember it was the strangest feeling. I didn't know what was wrong. I knew my mother was sitting beside the bed, and I knew who she was, but I didn't know who or where I was, and I was too afraid to ask my mama any questions. That night it was lightning, no thunder, just lightning. Heat lightning was what the adults called it. What made it so strange was that I was always afraid of lightning and would hide my face and try not to see it, but that night I was so numb to my surroundings that it didn't bother me. I know now that either I was in profound shock or I had endured all the traumatic depression my little eight-year-old mind and heart could bear. All my pain, hurts, and horrors I bore in silence. I never cried and I did not have anyone rescue me from the dark pit of hopeless despair and depression that I was in.

I was ready to give up on life and just go into the voided place, wherever that was. I was entirely beyond any ability to cope with all the sadness, hurt, grief, and loneliness that had been in my life for as long as I could remember. I was only eight years old, but I was experiencing the depth of depression. As I looked into the sky, the sky lit up with lightning and I saw the full face of Jesus. I'll never forget that moment as long as I live. I can still see it like it just happened yesterday or this morning. His face was blue and the lightning that surrounded his face was yellow with a little red mixed in. I can't explain the comfort that came over me. Jesus brought me back to reality and out of that period of depression. He gave me the strength to continue to endure all that I would have to experience to lead the ministry He would one day call me to lead.

Depression continued into adulthood and into a marriage that was never good for me. I was blessed to be adopted into the family of God in June of 1961 after the death of my six-week-old baby. Having salvation was the factor that enabled me to become a survivor. Sadness, inactivity, difficulty in thinking and concentration, and feelings of dejection continued to be a part of my life. I completed nursing school and held a full-time job, but the bouts of depression continued to become worse. I now had a husband and five children to care for while dealing with depression.

I had an excellent job as a nurse at one of the local hospitals, but I would go to work depressed. I would then go home, get my children off to school, and fall into bed and stay there for as long as I could. I would get up, feed my children, and then go back to bed until it was time to go back to work.

The time came when I was so depressed that I couldn't get up or function at all. All I wanted was to die and be out of my pain and misery. This landed me in the hospital on the psych ward again and again. Every time I felt better; my job would still be there. I was never questioned as to why I was losing so much time. I would be out anywhere from four to six weeks at a time, two to three times every year, for ten years. However, God was still in control! I was depressed but living in His GRACE. I can remember being so depressed that I couldn't even comb my hair. One day I came to the point where I felt dying was better than living. I also attempted to take my life two times. I was unable to think of what would happen to my five children when I was not there to take care of them.

Here is a description of one of those times...

On this day I somehow found the strength to clean my bedroom. I changed the bed and took a shower and put on one of my most beautiful nightgowns. I combed my hair and got ready to end my life. I had enough pills to kill five or six people and I intended to swallow every one that I had. I got a tall glass of water and told my little daughter not to wake mama and to stay in her bed until daddy got home. I knew by that time I would be dead. I sat on the side of my bed with the pills and the water beside me. When I went to pick up the pills and the glass of water, I did not have the strength in my hands to lift them. I thought to myself that maybe I had done too much so I needed to lie down and rest for a few minutes before I could take the pills. Well, as soon as my head touched the pillow, the Lord took me and I went down in a spiral. It was blacker than black. I went down and down! I don't know how far before I stopped. When I stopped, I was in a place so black I could feel it. I saw nothing, and I heard nothing, but God was there. I went into the thick darkness where God was and there was peace in that place that could not be explained. It was peace that you could feel. There was no fear, just that incredible peace. I have no idea how long I was there. I felt myself coming back up the spiral and when I opened my eyes, I felt so good. The depression for the moment was gone and the idea of taking my life was gone.

Things were good for a while, but then the depression came again because nothing in my life changed and the causative factors were still present in my life. The pain due to the depressive state can become so great that you will look for a way to escape. I reached that point and to numb myself to all feeling, I started using drugs (as a nurse at that time, it was not a difficult thing to do). I used all types of narcotics, not realizing that this action made the depression so much worse. There were days that I drove my car home and later wondered how I got home as sedated as I was. How did I function? I know it was God! When I say I used drugs, I mean I used drugs on a large scale! Discontinued drugs enabled me to take whatever I wanted. Although it was wrong, I didn't look at it as stealing because they would be destroyed anyway. This occurred from about 1944 – 1978. This period of my life was so dark that it is still somewhat of a blur in my mind. About 1978, I felt myself starting to go back into that severe depression. Somehow I knew that I couldn't live through another bout of that debilitating depression. One night I was so desperate that I knew I was going down for the count this time. I went to my bedroom, dropped to my knees, and cried from my heart (tears). I cried out to the Lord that I couldn't go through another spell of this depression. I knew that if I did, I would surely die! I was saved, but I had not learned to give my struggles entirely to God. I had finally come to the place where I realized that God was the answer to all I had tried to do on my own for over twenty plus years.

That night and at that very moment I got my miracle! God lifted that depression instantly, and I felt the weight come off of me when He did. I went to my dresser, got my pills, and then flushed every pill I had down the toilet. I have never had depression like that again, and I haven't taken a pill since. That was over forty years ago. I have learned that there are things I was and continue to be unable to handle in my strength. What is too large for me to handle, there is a God who will move mountains and will make the crooked paths straight—if I surrender to Him! What He has done and continues to do for me, He will do for anyone who will ask Him out of a sincere heart.

"Walking By Faith"

Chapter 6

Crystal's Struggle with Depression
(45 years old)

"It's your turn to read." "Oh no, I have to read in front of the class." My stomach churned. I began to fidget with my socks, hair, or whatever I thought would calm me. Eventually, I ended up in the Title 1 Reading class, not because I could not read, but because anxiety would set in. It would cause me to hesitate in my reading efforts, and it took me many attempts to read something. The Title 1 instructor was confused about how I ended up in the class because there was no issue with my reading ability. This was the beginning of my struggle with anxiety and I was only in the first grade. Every time I had to take a test at school, had to stand before my peers, or even the congregation at church, my stomach would end up in knots, and often I would end up in the bathroom. On test days I barely made it out of the house in time to catch the bus. I always strived to do my best, but sometimes the anxiety would not allow my best to shine through. As my elementary school years went by, I began to be bullied for being overweight and extremely shy. This only increased my anxiety and I started to have bouts of depression. Mental health was not something that African Americans even thought about at this time, so I struggled in silence.

Middle school was a little different. I lost weight and gained the attention of the cool kids. However, in the seventh grade, I had several life-changing events occur. There was a female gym teacher who was a little more than friendly. She was always making sly comments and trying to get some of us alone with her in the locker room. I did not realize that she was sexually harassing us. Then the unthinkable happened—I was raped by an ex-boyfriend. In the seventh grade, dating is supposed to be pure and innocent. I still remember the day like it was yesterday. We were at a school dance. "Hey, can you come talk to me?" he asked. "Sure," I said. We began to talk. Then he asked me to walk with him. My naivety did not see the harm in walking with him. This walk led to the back of the building, he pushed me against the door and started kissing me as he forced my pants down. I started screaming for help. Two of his friends appeared, but not to come to my rescue. They were there to be his protection to make sure he was not caught. It was over, finally. I was left alone when it was over. I walked back to the building where my friends were. I cried uncontrollably, but I could not tell them what happened. We had a sleepover that night at my friend's house so once we got there, I finally told them what had happened and they all laughed and started teasing me, saying things such as "that was your first time, ha, ha, ha?" and "Stop crying, it's no big deal." The next day I went home and tried to pretend nothing had happened; of course, I didn't want my parents to know. I was so depressed and lost after the rape, but I had no one to talk to. Everyone at school was laughing and teasing me. Eventually, another student tried to touch me and say inappropriate things to me. One day he touched me right before I was called to the chalkboard to complete a math problem. Then he started whispering vulgar things. At this point, I lost it. I threw the chalk down and said, "I am tired of this s***." I was immediately taken to the principal's office. I broke down and told the principal about the gym teacher and the bullying. I didn't talk about the rape at all because I was too ashamed and was trying to erase it from my memory. I was sent to the school psychologist immediately because I told the principal I wanted to kill myself. After this, I saw a psychologist several times but never divulged anything about being raped. My parents thought that I was just using the psychologist to get what I wanted since the psychologist encouraged them to allow me to do more extracurricular activities, not fully understanding the extent of my depression. I'm not sure why I only saw the psychologist for a few times, but I assume it was because my parents thought it was unnecessary. They felt I needed to embrace God more fully and everything would be alright. Things got better for a few years, but the depression and anxiety were still there. As I got older, I was able to develop and utilize coping skills. I remembered learning about journaling and began to journal even though, at the, time I did not realize how it was assisting me in my struggle. I also utilized my love for arts and crafts and always had a project to work on alone in my room, of course. I also found a passion for music and singing.

High school was pretty much uneventful. My anxiety decreased due to the coping skills that I started to utilize near the end of middle school. I was placed in the advanced reading class. This was a significant boost for my ego and proof that I should have never been in Title 1. One event that boosted my self-esteem was being accepted as a member of the school show choir. Participating in school show choir was another means to assist in overcoming my anxiety. I remember going to regional choir tryouts and being so nervous that I sounded like a dying cat. What a letdown. During this time, I did obtain some close friends and even a boyfriend who had the same beliefs as I did. We were at church all of the time. This was also when I began to study God's Word more and grew closer to Him.

My anxiety followed me to college. Attending class was no problem as long as the professor did not call on me to speak, but interacting with my peers outside of the classroom was impossible. Even though I was living on campus, I only went into the cafeteria two times the entire semester. The anxiety would hit me hard as I approached the cafeteria doors. I was always hungry. I lived off of saltine crackers and my roommate's butter that I would use once she left the room.

The relationship that I was in for over a year with my first love came to an end. I continued to hang out with the same friends that I obtained before entering college. However, the new crowd that we hung out with was not the most positive. I began dating, which lead me down a very bumpy rugged road for several years. I was looking for love in all the wrong places and became very promiscuous and thought this FALSE LOVE would heal my wounds. I began to drink alcohol daily, even before class. Depression was overtaking my life, but I did not have a label for it at this time. I fell away from God and also questioned His existence until I had a car accident that turned my life around. I was not injured in the crash, but the seat belt broke during the impact, and the paramedics had to use the Jaws of Life to remove me from the car. The only explanation for why I was not harmed was GOD!!! I left my friends and began to serve God with my whole heart, spending most of my time in church and helping others learn about Christ. My mother became my best friend, my only friend. She gave me all of the support and encouragement that I needed to thrive during this period in my life. I tried to encourage my old friends to give their lives to Christ as well, but they all thought it was a joke and that my change was only for a season. I was in the real world now and it was time to move out of my parents' home. My anxiety and depression were totally under control at this time. I eventually began working two jobs and attending graduate school full-time. This eventually led me back into a battle with anxiety. I was never entirely rested and struggled to stay awake in class. I was falling asleep so often in class that I felt the need to apologize to my professor, who was very understanding and gave me the encouragement I needed to move on. The supervisor at my full-time job pulled me to the side one day and told me if my lifestyle did not change I was going to end up in the hospital. I chose to quit graduate school. At this time my mental state must have been obvious to all who were around me.

On one snowy day while at this job, I was sitting on the bench waiting for a ride from the snow brigade and guess who came to sit beside me— the boy who raped me in the seventh grade. I had seen him many times over the years and even talked to him, but this time it was different. I lost it! I started screaming, "Why are you sitting near me? I hate you!" "What are you talking about? Have you lost your mind?" he asked. I then realized that he had no idea why I was acting out. The incident probably left his mind in the seventh grade. This caused another setback. This lead me deeper into my depression, but I kept silent once again. How can I tell anyone that I am depressed over something that happened over ten years ago? Instead, I started looking for love in all the wrong places again and had several other bad relationships.

Even though I was back to doing my "worldly things," I continued to attend church. It was the only thing that kept me from going over the deep end. I eventually ended up in a physically and verbally abusive relationship for four years. I befriended the guy at first because he had strayed from the church and God, and I wanted to help him. The next thing I knew, I was wrapped up in a relationship that I couldn't get out of. I did not realize how far he had strayed. He was a heavy drug user and had multiple relationships during the time we were together. I remember walking around with bruises on my body thinking this is okay because one day he will turn back into the nice guy he used to be. He went as far as to drag me while the car was moving one day, but that did not change my view of the situation at all. I ended up pregnant by him, and he insisted that I have an abortion. My depression was so great at this time I could barely function. I would go to work, lock myself in the bathroom, cry, come out, and pretend nothing happened. I confided in a friend at the church who told me it's no big deal; everyone she knew had had at least one, if not several abortions. Once again, I was questioning if something was wrong with me for being depressed over this life occurrence. Eventually, I did come out of the massive depression through confiding in a minister that I met during a women's conference. However, I did stay with this guy even after finding out that he had cheated on me numerous times throughout our relationship. We eventually made plans to get married. Everyone I knew was against this union. Even after I heard God speak in an audible voice telling me not to marry him, I continued with my plans. "God, are you for real? All of the plans are in order. I can't get embarrassed like that." My bridal shower was more like a prayer meeting to stop the wedding from happening. Eventually, this man did call the wedding off, saying he did not want to ruin my life. I can tell, THAT WAS GOD! My mother still thanks him to this day. After the breakup, I began to realize just how big and dark the cloud was that had been over my head for four years. The shadow of depression was lifted, and I began to live life again.

Close to a year after the end of that relationship, I met my husband. He was the total opposite of what I was used to dating. However, I was in fear of commitment, and he was also, due to the horrific relationships we both endured prior. We told each other that we were just looking for a friend to hang out with, nothing serious. We married after one year. After being married for over a year, the honeymoon was over. We began to argue over the smallest thing, not unusual for many marriages during this stage. However, since I dealt with depression many times in the past, it was easy for me to fall into that trap again. We were also in a blended family, which brought about many challenges that multiplied our problems. Through counseling with a couple of local pastors and our dedication to each other, we made it through. Three years into our marriage we decided it was time to start a family. I became pregnant, everything was going wonderfully. We were having a baby girl. One night I began to have pains and bleeding. I contacted the doctor. "This is nothing to be worried about. Just take it easy and prop your feet up." I woke up the next day in more pain, so I went to the hospital. This was Father's Day morning. They completed an ultrasound, and I saw my little girl doing her usual moving around like crazy. Then the doctor spoke, "I'm sorry but you are probably going to lose your baby, and it will be today." I began to scream and cry uncontrollably. The next thing I knew, the nurse came in with a sedative. They tried everything they knew to keep my little girl from coming, but today was going to be her birthday. God had a different plan from our plan. She was perfect in every way. Her grandparents and a few other family members had the privilege of meeting her before she passed later that day. I was under so much sedation that there are parts of the day that I don't remember. Leaving the hospital with a memory book and no baby was the hardest thing that I had ever done in my life.

The days ahead were filled with nothing but despair and depression. I sat around crying, didn't eat, and barely slept. The doctors prescribed antidepressants and scheduled me to see a psychologist in their office. I was reluctant to take the antidepressants because I felt like I was supposed to feel this way and needed nothing to take the edge off. My husband and I went to the first meeting with the psychologist and everything went well. I continued to take my medication; however, I felt like my emotions were being locked inside of my head. The second appointment came around. At the beginning of the session, the psychologist stumbled around trying to remember if I had a boy or girl. This infuriated me! "How can you help me if you didn't take enough time to read over my file before the session? Maybe it's no big deal to you, but my daughter meant the world to me." I left that day and never returned. This put a terrible taste in my mouth. I refused to seek any further assistance from professionals; however, God sent some powerful women to plant seeds of hope into my life. I eventually discontinued taking the antidepressants and was able to move forward and even try to conceive again. A little less than two years after having my daughter, I became pregnant again. My miracle twins! I had petitioned the Lord for twins after losing my daughter, and He answered my prayers. This time, a lot of precautions were taken to ensure that I remained pregnant as long as possible. I was on bed rest for six weeks. Bed rest in itself is extremely depressing. I had a list of scriptures that I studied and meditated on throughout the day when I started to get down. At twenty-five weeks, my water broke. I went to the hospital, and, once again, I was told, "We are sorry. You are probably not going to be able to carry them much longer. We are going to send you to a hospital in another city where you will have all of the medical care you need to carry them as long as possible, and where they can receive adequate care if they are born prematurely." During this time I struggled to maintain my sanity. The thought of my children being born this early, the possibility of losing them, and just the difficulty of being monitored and probed twenty-four hours a day sent me to a shallow point. One day I began sobbing, "I can't do this any longer." A nurse came into the room she said, "I know this is not my job and I could even get fired for this but, Can I pray with you?" She prayed with me and I felt a great release immediately both mentally and physically. My twins were born at twenty-six weeks. They remained in the hospital for several months and had many near-death experiences. I always say a mother that has endured having preemies and spent any time in the NICU should receive an award. There were days that I was excited and happy. When they had difficult days, I was sad and often scared. The roller coaster ride of the NICU made me a much stronger person. Near the end of their stay, I was able to regulate my emotions more efficiently. Little did I know that there was a new dilemma on the way, which would be caring for twins with special needs. The twins came home on oxygen, monitors, and lots of medication. Sleep was my least priority at this time. I began to use exercises and Weight Watchers as an outlet once they were healthy enough to venture out.

Years went by without any great bouts of depression or anxiety. I began to wake up every morning quoting the scripture, "I will bless the Lord at all times, and His praises shall continually be in my mouth. My soul shall make her boast in the

Lord: the humble shall hear thereof, and be glad (Psalm 34:1-2). I worked part-time and there were no significant stressors in my life. I eventually went back to the job that I had before the twins, but only part-time. I waited several years for a full-time position to come open. It never did, so I began applying for jobs to no avail. I either didn't have the perfect qualifications, or I let the anxiety get the best of me during the interviews. I remember one specific interview where I forgot the question in the middle of answering the question. I started sweating profusely, and then eventually my words turned to gibberish. I wanted to disappear at that point. After that interview, I vowed that I would not allow that to happen again. From that day on, before entering an interview, I would listen to music and utilize breathing exercises to regulate my stress.

After being unsuccessful in obtaining a job, I decided to return to school. Just filling out the application caused my anxiety to increase. The classes started off alright and I only had anxiety when test time came around. Eventually, the thought of reading and completing the assignment caused enormous stress, not to mention I was working a part-time job outside of the home, completing work for my business, and caring for my family. By the end of the first year, I was so depressed, but I knew this was one goal that I had to complete. I visited my doctor expressing my concerns. This was not only causing problems in my home because I was taking all of my frustrations out on my family, but it was also taking a toll on my health. I began to gain weight. It was gradual over time and caused by stress eating. Consequently, my blood pressure had also increased. The doctor suggested that I begin taking medication to assist with my anxiety and depression. I made it for two days and then decided I can do this without the medication. I just need to depend on God. I continued down this road of destruction in an attempt to fulfill my career goals for several more months. I went back to the doctor for a physical and had a mental breakdown right in her office. She insisted once again that I try taking medication to ease my anxiety and depression. I left the office thinking, "I have no choice this time. If I don't take this medicine, I may end up having a breakdown." I also heard my friend's voice telling me, "It's okay to take the medication. It does not mean that you are crazy. Sometimes you need assistance. It does not have to be permanent." I began taking the medication a week after the doctor's visit, but it was not soon enough. I started having breathing problems. By the next day, my breathing was so shallow that I ended up in the emergency room. After a battery of tests, they determined that it was probably the stress of everything that I was doing. I decided from that day on that I would eliminate as many stressors from my life as possible.

I stopped trying to be everything to everybody and began caring for myself. I felt like a different person on the medication. I no longer had anxiety when completing assignments or taking tests. I was no longer angry at the world and taking it out on my family. I thought, "Why didn't I take the medication sooner? My life would have been so much better without the continuous battle that was in my head." After completing my degree, I discontinued taking the medication, but not until I knew my life was at a place where I could manage without letting stress overtake my life.

"And we know that all things work together for good to them that love God, to them who are called according to his purpose" (Romans 8:28, KJV). This is a scripture that is commonly used when those of the faith are going through difficult situations. However, we must fully embrace this Word by realizing that "ALL THINGS" in healing mental health issues not only includes prayer, meditation on God's Word, studying the scriptures, godly counsel, and having faith, but also other resources, including counseling, medication therapy, and various forms of creative therapy. My life struggles with depression and anxiety have led me to a place where I fully understand my triggers and how to overcome them through "EVERYTHING" that God has created for my healing.

"Walking by Faith"

Chapter 7

Brittney's Struggle with Depression
(23 years old)

I believe that there is power in sharing your testimony. I was asked to tell my story. The journey to freedom has been grueling. On the other side, I realize that every step was worth it.

I was sexually abused as a child. I grew up with an excessive amount of emotional and verbal abuse. I allowed myself to be taken advantage of by boys throughout most of my teenage years. I have struggled with anxiety and depression for the majority of my life. I have struggled with cutting. I have fought through suicidal thoughts. I grew up around messages that reinforced the idea that I was unloved, unwanted, and without value. I built a dysfunctional set of beliefs about myself and the world around me. I was extremely distrusting and outraged. I lived my life in a dark cloud, only minimally experiencing the world around me. Experience taught me to reject emotion because it allowed me to temporarily reject pain. At the time, pain was the most prominent thing in my world. I frequently found myself gasping for air as anxiety had its fingers tightly wrapped around my throat and its weight was smashing my chest. I lived in a constant state of immense fear and worry. This was life as I knew it. I was unaware that there was a better life on the other side. I was content in this space because it was familiar to me. Let's use this as a starting point. This is where the journey began.

I grew up in the church. I was taught that God was good, that He protects and takes care of His children, and that He loved me. I heard these things so many times, but there could not have been a more significant disconnect in my heart. I could not perceive the goodness of God, especially because my reality did not line up with these truths. The events of my childhood did not preach that God was good. My constant struggle with anxiety and insecurity did not teach that God was good. As far as I was concerned, I was just trying to make it.

For the first couple of years of undergraduate, I remember pleading with the Lord to lift the weight of the pain in my heart. I said every prayer, I read as many books as I could, I listened to countless sermons, and I went to every deliverance session I could attend. I tried all that I could to fill the void in my heart. I was tired of living in pain. Toward the end of that span of time, I sat down with a friend and explained the internal battle that I had been fighting, expecting the release of my emotions and the momentary transparency to change something in my heart. At that point, I had so many secrets that were kept in the depths of my heart. There was a library of hurt that was archived deep within the recesses of my soul. Even as I cracked the door to the vault, I was only physically capable of divulging an insufficient amount of information. I was proud of the courage to be voluntarily vulnerable for one of the first points in my lifetime. At the same time, I was petrified that I was allowing someone else to see the real me. I quivered at the fear of judgment and at the thought of what my vulnerability would do to the relationship. As I stumbled to the end of my story, that friend graciously told me that I needed to seek help and that she had the resources to offer if I was willing to take them. At the moment, I was completely offended that she thought that I needed the help of a professional. Over the course of the next couple of days, I realized that I needed help, and I made a call to a local counseling office.

Making the call and showing up for my first appointment took an immense amount of bravery.

Looking back, I believe it was the grace of the Lord that got me there. I was filled with fear. Taking that step meant challenging what I had lived with for twenty-two years of my life. It said gaining the courage to step outside of the cloud of depression, not knowing what was outside of it. I was terrified, but I showed up. At that point, I knew that I needed help, but I was not entirely willing or able to do the work that was required to become well. There were things that I had never told another human being, and I fully intended to keep it that way. There were places and memories that I had no intentions of touching. I did not know that I would eventually have to surrender these things. I committed to the journey without the willpower and the tools to successfully carry it out. I developed those things along the way. Beginning the process took a simple "yes." I wanted something different for my life, and I was ready to start making the changes necessary to make it happen. Making it to the end of that road required that I keep saying "yes" to remembering the goal, trusting the process and doing all of the uncomfortable things that stretched me.

One of the most significant components of this journey was learning a healthy identity. In the process, I found that there was a caveat about learning about who I was. As humans, we were created by God to be in relationship with Him. All that we are is an offshoot of this original intention. Without knowing the heart and the character of the Creator, it was impossible for me to understand my true identity. I am created by a loving Creator for His enjoyment; therefore, I am loved, I am cherished, and I am valued. When I first started the process of healing, I had no connection to these messages. So throughout the transition, I had to revise my entire mindset. So, if my experiences did not preach the goodness of God, it did not mean He was not good. It said that I misunderstood. If life is a puzzle, it is mpossible to assume the rest of the picture from the depiction of a couple of connected pieces. The image on the related parts may be clear, but that image is only a slight indication of the bigger picture. In my experiences, I made many value statements and conclusions about the character of God with my understanding of only a few pieces. A big part of my growth was putting new language to the history bank of my past.

This step radically changed my life. It influenced my thought process, it altered the way that I interacted with people, and it affected the way that I thought. Though the process was a tremendous impetus for change, my external circumstances changed very little. There was not any exchange of earth-shaking apologies. The people in my relationships changed very little. This realization broke my heart and the way that I interacted with the world. In the most descriptive sense, this journey was a battle. Before starting the process, I lived my life as if I was fighting the darkness. I thought that I was always in a struggle with depression, anxiety, and with every evil force that mounted itself against me. In reality, Christ had already won that battle for me on the cross. Being His meant that the darkness was already defeated for me. As a believer, that was my rightful inheritance. Why fight battles that you have already won? So the journey was a process of coming to understand my identity and place as a victor, not a victim. Changing my belief systems and frameworks ultimately influenced my interaction with anxiety and depression. It took almost two years to sort through all of my mess. But when I got to the end of the road, I realized that I was no longer in the cloud that I had spent my entire life inside of. Life felt comfortable and light. For the first time, I experienced the fullness of joy. Although I could not change my external environment, I learned how to change my perspective on the conditions I faced. Being able to perceive the goodness of God in every situation is necessary for a sound mind and a clear direction of your days ahead and your outlook on life. In the beginning, all of the affirmations I would tell myself were merely theory, but they became deeply rooted beliefs that lifted the weight of anxiety off of my shoulders. Freedom was the most significant gift I have ever received. It felt like salvation. It was crazy knowing that this was God's original intention for me all along. The gospel had radically transformed all that I was.

I have tasted and seen that the Lord is good. When I sit and think of the goodness of God and His love for me, I quickly become overwhelmed. He had His hand on my life. There were so many points that were catastrophic for me and almost destroyed me, but He rescued me because He delighted in me. His grace is incredibly apparent to me, and His freedom is the most significant gift that I have ever known. It is my joy to lay everything at His feet. This entire journey has been for the pursuit of understanding Him. Every single road has led to Him. More so, the whole journey was Him winning my heart, piece by piece and bit by bit. It is the greatest love story ever told.

Looking back through some of the journals I wrote throughout the process, I was asked to write a letter to my younger self. I included it with the hope that my readers will find encouragement to do hard things and to face the deepest of their fears.

"Letter To My Younger Self"

My sweet one,
Beautiful, headstrong, bold. You have not even reached the beginning. I could tell you how bright your future is. I could tell you that the wounds of your heart will heal. I could tell you that you will soon have a community that will love you well. I could tell you that you will

meet guys who are not pigs, ones who will treasure your heart. But would you believe in the weight of truth in my words? Would the power of my words be enough to cause a shift in your heart? If only you knew that you are loved. You are cared for. You are wanted.

If only I had the words to change the infrastructures of your belief systems completely. For that, I would give fortunes. But if I had to boil it all down to one statement, I would tell you, "Keep pushing for just a little while longer. It's coming."

Experience is the teacher of the neglected. He is faithful, but there is one who is far more faithful. His Helper will lead you into the paths of truth. He will direct healing light on the deepest of your wounds. It is coming; just push a little while longer.

The Promised Land of your heart is on the horizon. Contrary to what you believe, it is not a land of perfection. Everything in this land is the opposite of what you have been taught; it counteracts the principles of the world. Love reigns there. Peace and joy dwell in its midst. Did you know that peace and joy are your portions? In just a little bit, they will be things that your heart knows well. It is an inside-out, upside-down Kingdom, it will change everything you know is right. Taste and see; its fruits are genuine and lavish. A *love for life and who you are will permeate the depths of your soul. Satisfaction with life is on the horizon. It is yours, and it is coming.*

In the pressing, you will get to know a Friend. He is faithful to you, and He seeks to win your heart. You should know that the process is laborious and requires the complete surrender and laying down your desire to be comfortable. Two things: first, your Friend will never leave your side; He fully delights in the process. It is the most significant love story you will ever know. And second, the journey is the best investment, and your returns will be richly profitable. You should not attempt to journey on alone; the sweat of your brow will never get you there.

You have a lot to look forward to, but there is undiscovered gold on the inside of you. Let's just say there is a man who searches the whole earth to find a definite, one-of-a-kind gem. He knows it exists and is so aware of the gem's value that he devotes his entire life to the pursuit. In the last days of his life, he finds the gem. Can you imagine the joy that resounds in his heart when he finally attains his treasure? All of his labor would be validated. Would you believe me if I told you that you are worth far more than that gem? Would you believe me if I told you that life was spent for the pursuit of who you are?

You are worth more than all of these things. You deserve to be loved and honored as the treasure that you are. There is beauty in the pushing. So, keep pushing, my love. You are almost there.

"Walking By Faith"

Chapter 8

Debra's Struggle with Depression
(61 years old)

Looking back at my past behaviors, I realize that even as a tiny young girl, I often felt very down and suffered from low self-esteem. I wanted to be accepted. When I was young, I often was teased about my body being small and underdeveloped, especially having "skinny legs."

In the third grade, we were all playing on the playground naming our daddies. To my surprise, a girl that was playing with us named my father. I was totally devastated. This brought about feelings of sadness and not being good enough to even be my daddy's baby girl. I was so upset. My dad worked second shift, and I waited for him to come home from work that night to ask him if he was her father. He was honest with me and said,

"Yes." At that point, I was in my room crying and feeling ashamed of being teased by the other kids in my class about this. I isolated myself from others and experienced feelings of hopelessness. I never talked to anyone during this time about how I was feeling or what was happening at school because of the embarrassment. When I entered the sixth grade, I was introduced to my first drinking experience and marijuana. Oh yes, I liked it, and it made me feel so accepted and confident, and I no longer felt ashamed about any of my body image concerns. Suddenly, I was feeling good enough. I was able to act secure and confident, and the substances had made those feelings go away that I had been having on the inside for years.

I became popular once I made the cheering squad. They accepted me, skinny legs and all. I finally felt like I fit in. Then, I met and fell in love with the football star in the 9th grade. We were both getting high. In 10th grade, he started using a different drug from me and began using heroin. He also became physically abusive. I was 15 years old and in an abusive relationship. I kept the fact that I was being abused by him a secret. My spirit was down, but I put on a mask of the popular and confident girl.

One Sunday afternoon in my parents' home, he slapped me in my dining room. I snapped and grabbed a knife and cut him. That is when my parents found out about what I had been hiding and lying about for several years. During this time of keeping secrets, I had several thoughts of suicide. I left Lynchburg the day after I graduated from high school. I went to college, but I didn't know that I was taking myself with me everywhere I went. In my household, God was a major part of our life, but I did not have my relationship with Him. The perception that I had was that God was punishing me. My substance abuse continued and progressed. I became like a shell, but I completed college and, by God's grace, did well academically. I even joined a sorority. I got married and had two beautiful children. My marriage lasted 19 years and, for 15 of those years, it was all good until the drugs and the lifestyle became more important to both of us than our family. I had several moments of total depression and emotional pain. During this time, my isolation was very intense. I never was diagnosed with depression because my drug use was a great coping mechanism that covered up a lot of what I was feeling.

I separated from my husband and moved back home to Lynchburg, VA, and continued to use drugs. I got into legal troubles which caused my family embarrassment. I developed feelings of hopelessness and depression, but I just could not stop using. I told myself a thousand times, "I can't keep doing this." I was granted the gift of mercy on August 5, 1993, while in jail. I fell to my knees and asked God to "please help me." My life changed, and I have been clean and in recovery for 24 years.

Life was good and healing was wonderful. My relationship with my family was improving. All was well.

I even remarried and was with my husband for almost 20 years when, in 2013, he said that he wanted out of our marriage. This was a significant blow to my life. I found myself many nights in a fetal position, which was very familiar to me. Yes, once again, I found myself in a dark place feeling suicidal and hopeless. But this time, I was a professional working in the mental health field, and I was drug- and alcohol-free. This is not supposed to be my story. In the past, I would have turned to drugs. I did not know what to do or how to get through this being sober. The only source I could depend on was God, and His grace was sufficient. There were some hard days, but He carried me through them. I sought medical help, and I did take an antidepressant for a while to help me get through the emotional pain that I was feeling. I had experienced a lot of grief and loss, and they were back to back. In a small time span, I lost both parents, and my 2 brothers-in-law. My sister suddenly passed away, and my nephew was killed by his wife. It was one emotional and painful incident after the other. But God. I am so thankful to God that my faith and my trust in

Him had grown. Even though I was screaming, praying, and crying for several months, I did not use any substances. I trusted in the Lord and used my support system of friends and family that God graced me with.

Once again, God's grace and mercy embraced me on May 26, 2016, when I was awakened at 5:30 am with chest pains and profuse sweating. I had a heart attack and survived. What I know is God loves me and He is so amazing. He is not finished with me yet, and there is indeed a purpose and call on my life. My story is, through all of the emotional pain, depression, and addiction, God has always protected and saved me through it all. He has even allowed me to be in a profession to reach back and pay it forward for others who have addiction, struggles, mental health issues, and hopelessness. Look at God!!! Only God can do this. Turn a mess into a message. Thank you, God, for your tender reminder that you are always with me and have always gone before me in all of the situations and circumstances in my life. We can all be lifted above our circumstances!!!

"Walking By Faith"

Chapter 9

Chenille's Struggle with Depression

(18 years old, name changed)

I am a freshman in college, and I started battling anxiety and depression when I was in middle school. I am one of 3 children, and I am the oldest. I was a tall kid and I was taller than most boys in my class, so I always felt uncomfortable about being tall. I was also the smart kid and the teacher called on me constantly. I knew all the answers, which did not cause me to be popular. In fact, I guess I was a nerd. I was bullied by other kids who would call me names like, "Giant Bitch, Elephant, Treetop, and Giraffe." I never told anyone for fear that it would make it worse for me and it was only two kids mainly. I just retreated within myself. I would often feel alone in a room full of people. I thought if I just sit still and not say anything then no one would notice me and no attention would be placed on me. So I stopped speaking up in class and I became the quiet kid. When the teacher called on me, I stumbled with answering the questions. Being the quiet kid was easy and it stopped the bullies from bullying me. They moved on to someone else. Looking back, I wish I would have had the nerve to tell someone what I went through but I was afraid and fearful. I did not think that remaining silent permitted them to continue hurting other people. I was a kid who had been so active in participating in music and dance, and then I lost interest in those activities. I retreated to my room and reading books and throwing myself into my school work. Very few things excited me and I had no interest in things that I had once enjoyed. I had limited interaction with people. I made myself eat, but I did not have much of an appetite which resulted in me losing weight. My mom thought I was just shedding my "baby fat." I had one teacher say to me, "You seem so different, are you ok?" I wanted to scream at the top of my lungs, "No I am not okay, I am sad!" Instead, I said, "I am good." I could be in a room full of people and feel alone or like I did not fit in. I felt like people were looking at me and talking about me. My mind was able to tell me that no one was talking about me, but it did not erase the physical feelings that I felt, which caused increased heart rate and racing thoughts. Sometimes, I would break out into a sweat and my hands would be sweaty. I felt like I could not breathe and often needed to go outside to breathe. It was a terrifying feeling because I did not know if I was dying or what was happening. Thank God it did not happen often. My mom was a single mother and my dad was in and out of our lives. He was not consistent, which also added to what I was dealing with. My mom was a hard worker and she worked to make things happen for us despite the inconsistency of my dad not being around. We knew we were loved and cared for but sometimes because of the lack of finances, I worried about how my mom would provide for us. She always said, "The Lord will make a way somehow." She was a strong Christian mother who taught us to pray about everything. Ever since I can remember we always attended church, vacation bible school, and summer camp at church. During this time I attended church because my mom made me but my mind was usually not on what the preacher was saying, I was usually thinking, "When is this going to be over so I can get back home?" I retreated to the car immediately after church, so I did not have to interact with anyone. I kept my struggles with depression to myself because I did not want my mother to have an added worry. My mother often checked in with me and asked, "Are you okay." I responded, "Yes, Mom I am fine." It's as if she suspected something, but I put my big smile on for her and would say, "Things are great." It hurt so much not to tell her what I had been dealing with. She often tried to engage me in conversation, but I always reassured her that I was fine and there was no need to worry. I would often hear her praying for me specifically in her prayers for God to protect my mind and cover me. I entered high school and things got better, but I noticed when I got overwhelmed, my anxiety and depression kicked in. So what did my life look like? Well, I went to school, my grades were good and I even had friends, but something was missing. There was a dark cloud hanging over me, and sometimes I felt like the cloud fell and rested on me. At those times, I felt excessive worry and paranoia. I would close my eyes and pray and it would lift. Sometimes I would be so down, and the emotional pain would cause me to cut myself for relief. I started this because it felt like I was releasing the pain and it made me feel better. I cut on my thigh because it was not obvious and no one would know. I never had a plan to kill myself, but I sometimes wondered how life would be without me—If I would even be missed, if anyone would even care, or if I was gone, if it would be easier for my mom to have one less mouth to feed. I was in my room cutting one day when I heard a small quiet voice say, "What are you doing?" I jumped up and ran to the door but no one was there. I proceeded to resume cutting, and I heard it again. I said, "God are you talking to me?" I fell to my knees and begin to pray, cry, and repent. I asked God to remove this feeling. I said, "God, I trust you and I love you. I believe that you died for me and I want to serve you. Please take away the pain and make me new. My life is yours. At the time, I was in high school around the 11th grade, and I had a spiritual encounter with God. That night I went to my mom and I told her everything that I had experienced and I opened up to her about how depressed and down I was. We stayed up all night talking, crying, and praying. My mother was so supportive and kept saying, "I wish you had told me." She shared with me that she had prayed for me but had no idea that I was going through so much emotional pain. The next day she scheduled an appointment for me with a Christian Counselor. I attended sessions with her once a week. She was awesome; she did not push me but worked with me on setting my own personal goals. She prayed with me during our sessions, and I was able to release a lot of past hurts. I really felt that God delivered me that night, but the rest was a process toward me learning to love myself and seeing myself as God sees me. Fast forward to today—I am a college freshman and I am enjoying my life. I still see a counselor who is more like my life coach. I am active in college clubs, and I exercise daily and monitor my diet. I am enrolled in a social work program and I pray that I will be able to use my experience to offer others hope that things can get better and that God is real.

Chapter 10

Tiera's Struggle with Depression
(29 years old)

As of this writing, I am 29 years old. I've lived a whole 29 years and then some. Living with and overcoming a demon that many (so, so many) battle and sadly lose against. I remember often being afraid that I would lose too. There were moments in my life that were so much darker than others, and each time social media or the news reported a death by suicide, I would fear for my own life.

WHAT IF? "What if" was the question. What if I became super bold one day and just…did it?

As Christians, we often pray for boldness. We cry out and we ask God for strength. "God, give me boldness! Give me strength!" we might say. I assure you, in this case, I really didn't need that.

To be honest, the one time I tried...well, we'll go over that later.

What's funny is I was actually afraid of death. Very much so. I don't like pain and shiver or grimace at the thought of it...but there were some days where I was so overwhelmed in my own thoughts and emotions that the only logical solution was to hurt myself in some way. There were days I craved to break something, to hurt something, or to hurt **me**. The anger I felt toward myself brought on that desire. There were days when I thought death would be much better than life. Why? Because only in death could I escape the myriad of emotions I felt and the frustration with my life's path.

I felt that people looked at me a certain way and I thought that if I told anyone, many wouldn't believe me. They probably would be shocked to know that in first grade I wrote a journal entry and described how I wanted to kill myself with a picture of what I would do—red blood included. That was sent home and was handled as best as it could be handled. Questions like "WHY!?" were asked..."I don't know," was the answer. How can you truly know at that age?

Baby Girl

I grew up as the only girl in my house, the baby of 5 between my mom and dad, and also had an older half-sister who grew up with her mom. It was what people would call a "broken home" in many ways. They would fight often and she would throw him out, let him come back, throw him out, and so forth. There wasn't much stability there and that would affect me for years.

Not only was there a lack of stability but there was a lack of warmth, affection, understanding, and love. I mean, I'm sure my mother loved me, but I just couldn't feel it and as a little girl, you need that from your mom. You need that affection, that comfort, that encouragement, and that strength. Otherwise, you can grow up with dire need of it—a void that we often try to incorrectly and sometimes, disastrously, fill.

At the age of 12, I was diagnosed with depression. While in the doctor's office one day, I noticed a questionnaire that asked about your feelings and mood and things of that nature. It intrigued me and as my mother and I waited for the doctor to return to the exam room, I took it upon my 12-year-old self to fill it out. I really had no idea what would come of this but when the doctor returned, she noticed it. She asked me questions like, "What are you doing depressed?" and asked my mom some questions as well. I admitted to being kept close, sheltered, if you will. I couldn't do the things other 12-year-olds do. She admonished my mother to let me have a social life and prescribed an antidepressant for me.

The truth was...though I was often perceived as jolly and giggly on the outside, my insides were all gray and cold. My mother was very overprotective and paranoid yet unaffectionate. She often pushed me away because she didn't do hugs (it was too hot for all that). Even more, I didn't hear the words, "I love you" until much later in life—long after the time I really needed it—and by then I didn't even want to hear it. It was uncomfortable and foreign to me. This caused me to hurt and build up so many walls I practically lived in an invisible fortress.

The Failure

For years I suffered off and on with depression. I knew I was different and that something was wrong but too often "we" don't talk about it. It's like we're afraid of being open and honest about our pain and shortcomings. But how can we overcome what we don't confront? What are we afraid of?

As I grew older and experienced the woes of adulthood, I felt so weak and unequipped. While my mother shielded me from the world, it must have slipped her mind to teach me some life skills. It seemed like everything was hard for me, and I seemed to "fail" over and over again, at one point, losing my job and my apartment. With increased responsibility and not knowing how to properly cope with it, depression increased. Here and there I had taken antidepressants and sought therapy on occasion but unfortunately neglected to maintain the treatment long-term.

As I said before, I always felt that I was different and would have particular difficulty in certain areas of my life. School and work were hard and staying focused was my enemy. I would struggle with prayers or reading or simply staying on topic in conversation. It was a continuing frustration for me and, at 27, I began to seek answers.

Following an evaluation by a psychologist, my suspicions were proved to be correct. I was found to have **ADHD Inattentive Type** and BOY, what a relief it was! Oftentimes, people see a diagnosis as a bad thing or a death sentence, but for me it was light. After all these years, it gave me a better understanding of myself and placed me on a path of healing.

That was just the first step of many on the path to my healthy place. Even with that huge relief I was still in the midst of one of the darkest depressive episodes in my life. Everything was stressful—work, church, and even thinking or praying sometimes stressed me out. It all seemed so hard. I thought about suicide often and whenever it would get really bad, I would write on myself to curb the urge to slice on myself or worse. If people were paying attention, they would often see scriptures such as Psalm 118:17 that says, "I shall not die, but live, and declare the works of the Lord" written on my arm or wrists. I at least knew to go back to the word and cling to it with everything in me—oftentimes repeating it to myself through anxiety, tears and sleeplessness.

I wanted to live but the pull of the supposed freedom of dying was all too strong. You may hear many suffering with mental illness say they really don't want to die, they just want the pain to stop. That was me...I just wanted it to **stop**.

Butterfly Season

Taking matters into my own hands, I took a leave from my job and searched for help. After some hits and misses I found a godsend of a place called Tucker Wellness & Recovery—an extension of HCA Chippenham Hospital Tucker Psychiatric Pavilion—that offered an outpatient partial hospitalization program (PHP). Their sole purpose is to teach coping strategies for behavioral health challenges, such as depression, anxiety, or stress and help you on your way to recovery. Not knowing what to expect, I entered into a place where no one would tell me I was making it up or to just get over it. The structured but comforting and inviting atmosphere totally changed my life. After almost 2 weeks, I walked out of there, sad to leave, but excited to embrace this new life that had suddenly opened up for me. It was like a new butterfly emerging from its cocoon with no choice but to fly.

The way I viewed life totally changed. Everything seemed new, and I realized that though I had been diagnosed with these mental illnesses they did not define me and it was absolutely possible to recover. What followed was an arduous process of ups and downs, continuous learning, and a coming to terms with the lot I had been given. I learned to forgive and let go of things that once had control over me. I had to be honest with myself and dig deep to address old wounds that had been covered up before or overlooked.

One of the biggest aspects of this was addressing the pain of rejection. For a long while, I didn't have a name for it, I just knew it hurt. I later learned that it affected me in so many ways, from the way I interacted with others, to the way I treated myself. I learned to forgive my mother for not giving me what she didn't have and to forgive others whose words and actions tore me down over the years. Literally, I was becoming a new creature in Christ and allowing God's passion, love, and grace toward me work its power.

As I was becoming free, I began gaining the confidence to step out and do things that I would have been scared to do before. Instead of finding excuses to why "I can't," I just did it. Starting a business was one of them.

Step by step, day after day, week by week, God would work in me and reveal more of myself to me. Each time I would overcome a thing, before long—and before I could celebrate too much—He would show me something else about me that I needed His help with. While it was painful at times, it was also necessary every time. I became a willing participant in my own healing and invited God to work in and heal every part of me.

The greatest part of this is knowing that God always had a plan for me. It's one of those things that you know, but you don't always want to admit to, and that is, **what you go through is not always for you but it's to help someone else**. What was most painful for me could be used to ensure someone else's victory. And, with that in mind, I purposed to posture myself unselfishly to be a support to others who may be in crisis.

If I may backtrack a bit, there was a period of time a few years before—some time in 2013—that had taken me to a dark place. I disappeared from work for over a week and just wallowed in it. It finally came to a head one night when I entered my kitchen, grabbed a knife, and steeled myself to "do the deed." With knife in hand, I was poised and finally ready, or so I thought, to take my own life. But then, out of the quietness of night, a resounding **"NO!"** rang out in my spirit and I knew right then to put that knife down. I didn't always audibly hear from God, but I knew His voice when I heard it. It was then that God intervened and reminded me that my life is not my own and I truly belong to Him. My life was not mine to take, and I had to complete my purpose here.

I am here to testify that we can make all the plans in the world for our life, but God's plans supersede them all...and that's Bible. Proverbs 16:9 to be exact. Never in a million years would I have thought of myself being on this path, but here I am: a business owner, a minister, a soon to be recovery coach and HEALED!

There's more to come and I owe God ALL.

Chapter 11

Walking By Faith

Hebrews 11:1 says, "Now faith is the substance of things hoped for and the evidence of things not seen." The women in the stories in this book each hoped that things would get better during the dark times. It may have appeared hopeless, but they relied on their belief that things would get better if they kept on going—that's faith. You may not see a way out, but you believe that a better day is coming. What if Lucille, Crystal, Brittney, Debra, Chenille, Tiera, or I would have given up on life? What if we would have just stopped on the journey and said, "I can't go on. Life is too hard." We would have missed the opportunity to share with the world what God has done in our lives. We would have missed the chance to help other women who find themselves in similar situations know that it does get better. It's not an easy journey to walk through depression, but with the right support and help, you can make it. The stories that you have read in the previous chapters are each from the perspective of a Black woman who struggled with depression. It is important to note: depression is not a spiritual deficit, the result of a lack of faith, or sin in your past. Depression can happen to anyone regardless of age, race, or gender. However, for the purpose of this book, I focused on the personal struggles of Black women because of my own experience and the silence and stigma I have witnessed in my community. Regardless of your race, gender, or economic status, the treatment recommendations in this book are the same for anyone who struggles with depression.

Walking out of depression takes courage. One must first admit that there is a problem in order to seek a solution to make it better. It takes courage to continue to move forward when you are emotionally in pain and in a dark place in life. 1 Corinthians 13:12 says, "For now we see through a glass darkly; but then face to face; now I know in part; but then shall I know even as also I am known." In other words, things may not make sense right now in your life; the puzzles may not fit together, and you may say, "Why am I going through this?" but take courage and think that one day all the puzzles will fit together and it will make sense. I believe that everything we go through is used by God for our good. The key is staying on the path and moving forward. Remember, in your darkest hours, God is there. He promises never to leave us nor forsake us, and even when you cannot feel or see Him in your situations, know that He is there. He understands your depression and will walk beside you through it with each step you take. Lao Tzu is quoted as saying, "The journey of a thousand miles begins with one step." It's important to keep on walking, just like each of my sista friends and I did and continued to do. We did not give up or in. We relied on our faith to strengthen and sustain us to keep walking on the path before us. For some of us, that path took us to see a doctor, therapist ,and yes, medication. We continued to walk until the darkness was dispelled by light.

Sure, there were times that we might have felt like God was not present in our suffering, but we continued to seek Him for direction on how to respond to our depression. Looking back, each woman admits He was with them the whole time. Each story was unique, but the standard thread in each of our stories was and still is our belief in God and our ability to press through the pain by getting the help and support we needed. Our faith in God provided us with the strength to believe that we could and would overcome the dark times. It was in our relationship with God that we sought answers. Individually, the stories are different, but collectively, they tell the story of many women who find themselves experiencing or battling depression. A story full of faith, hope, and resiliency.

Have you ever experienced stressors such as anxiety, depression, worry, or guilt to the point that you felt like you were consumed by it? Maybe the source of these feelings came from being on drugs, a mentally/ physically abusive relationship, the death of a loved one, or perhaps you experienced some trauma. You may have felt like your life was spiraling out of control and you had no peace of mind and found it hard to focus. You may have been at a point where you wanted to pray but were unable to pray. Everything that you knew to do became distant and remote and you lacked the energy or the mindset to do what was right, so you gave into the feelings of hopelessness and despair. Maybe your thoughts were dark and flooded with ideas of self-harm or thoughts that maybe you would be better off dead than alive. Perhaps you lost your mind for a moment or had a psychotic episode. Whatever your story is, if you are currently in the midst of this dark moment right now, know that there is hope, and it is found in a relationship with Jesus, who will direct your path to recovery and restore your mind. If God has brought you through, or is bringing you through, there is a reason to thank Him for keeping you in your right mind. The alternative to not being in your right mind is your inability to make decisions for yourself. Most of these people are harmful to themselves or others, and they require psychiatric inpatient treatment. For some, it may be a temporary loss of sanity because of the stressors that have pushed one to the point of no longer thinking or acting in a manner that is healthy to self or others. At this point, some may not even realize that they are in the world or able to control what is happening around them. You may be wondering how one gets to this point. It can happen so quickly, and it's important to note that it happens with individuals who are in the church all the time. Have you ever been so angry or depressed that you could have very well just committed suicide or homicide? These are the times that we could have lost our minds or maybe we did. Somewhere on your journey, you had to admit that you were powerless but God was all-powerful, and you had to "sit at His feet" and listen to Him for direction on improving your life. You had to allow Him to be God in your life and surrender your will and let His will be done in your life. It does not matter how you got your deliverance. The important thing is that you were/ are restored to wholeness. Everyone's journey is different, but the one thing that connects us is our faith. If we trust God and listen to Him and follow the leading of the Holy Spirit, we will make the right decisions for our mental health.

Chapter 12

Restoration and Recovery— Seeking Professional Help

The first step in getting help is admitting that you have a problem. I think this is the hardest step because often we try hard to convince ourselves that we don't have a problem. We replay the messages in our head from the past, and we put a lot of emphasis on what others will say or think. It's not easy to walk into a counselor or doctor's office and start sharing your feelings. Sometimes, all it takes to begin the process of healing is to talk it out with another person. Pastors can serve in this role, but they need to be educated to know how far they can go and when to refer to a licensed professional counselor. For pastors, this is not an admission that you can't help, but the person may require more intensive help.

Medication is not the answer for everyone; a person may not need it. In looking for a counselor, consider counselors who are Christian counselors. Check them out thoroughly and read their reviews. You want someone with whom you feel a connection and feel safe. If you attend a session and you don't have a good feeling, don't continue to go—follow your gut. I believe God will give you a spirit of discernment on what you need as far as choosing a counselor and taking the right medications as well. Consider attending a support group for people who are struggling with depression. These types of groups are listed in the local newspaper, or you can google online for the local support group. If you cannot afford to pay for counseling services, each locality should have a community-based counseling service that will provide free or sliding scale fee services.

If you or someone you know is in crisis and is a harm to themselves, or others call 911 (police) for help. There is help available, but it requires reaching out and taking the first step.

People do get better, but it requires a person to work through a recovery plan that works for them.

Each person's treatment is individualized, but help is available to meet his/her needs. It is essential to stay active, exercise, eat a proper, balanced diet, and get adequate sleep and rest. Physical health parallels with mental health, and one would be amazed how just drinking water and eating nutritious meals can change the way one feels.

Chapter 13

What Can "You" Do?

Many times I am asked by family members and friends, "What can we do to help our loved one who is struggling with mental health or addictions?" You can educate yourself on mental health disorders. We know knowledge is power. Be supportive and loving. If you or someone you know is struggling, get help. If you see them struggling and they do not want help, monitor their behavior and check in on them often. If they are a harm to themselves or others, get the police involved or get the person evaluated at the local hospital. An efficient support system for helping a person with a mental health disorder is crucial and affects the recovery process. You can start to speak out. The more people begin to share and talk about their mental health issues, the more it chips away at the stigma. Have the discussion in your small groups at church; when planning health fairs, include mental health as a part of the festival; and sponsor programs that have psychiatrists, counselors, and persons who are recovering from mental health issues to come and share. Use this book in your women's ministry or group to start the discussion on mental health restoration and recovery.

Questions for Small Group Discussion

- *Read the scripture Mark 5:15 and discuss the interpretation of the scripture and what it means to be "clothed and in his right mind."*

- *When you hear the words mental health, what comes to mind?*

- *Why do you think Black women don't talk about their mental health?*

- *Discuss each woman's story? What are some signs that these women were experiencing depression?*

- *Have you ever experienced depression? If yes, share with the group how you chose to deal with your depression.*

- *Do you have family or friends who suffer*

from depression? If yes, have you been supportive of them? How?

- *What role do you think the faith community can play in addressing mental health in the church? What can you do?*

- *Come up with an action plan for addressing mental health in your church/community in the next year. (i.e., awareness programs; observing Mental Health Awareness Month; inviting a psychiatrist, licensed professional counselor, or a person in recovery to speak; supporting local mental health organizations and partnering with them on programs; establishing a health ministry that addresses physical and mental health.)*

About the Author

Mrs. Rhonda Fuller Turner, a native of Chatham, Virginia, is currently residing in Staunton, Virginia, with her husband, Reverend Doctor Michael A. Turner, Sr. She is the "bonus mom" to stepchildren Michael Anthony, II, and Florin Michaela. She is the daughter of John and Mozelle Fuller. Rhonda is a licensed, ordained minister, who serves with her husband in ministry. She attended Norfolk State University, Lynchburg College, and Liberty University. She is a Certified Substance Abuse Counselor with the Commonwealth of Virginia and a National Certified Master Addiction Counselor. Rhonda has over twenty years of experience working with substance use and mental health disorders.

 RHONDA FULLER TURNER

Scripture References for Support (Amplified Version)

Matthew 11:28-30: "Come to Me, all who are weary and heavily burdened [by religious rituals that provide no peace], and I will give you rest [refreshing your souls with salvation]. Take My yoke upon you and learn from Me [following Me as My disciple], for I am gentle and humble in heart, and you will find rest (renewal, blessed quiet) for your souls. For My yoke is easy [to bear] and My burden is light."

Philippians 4:6-7: Do not be anxious or worried about anything, but in everything [every circumstance and situation] by prayer and petition with thanksgiving, continue to make your [specific] requests known to God. And the peace of God [that peace which reassures the heart, that peace] which transcends all understanding, [that peace which] stands guard over your hearts and your minds in Christ Jesus [is yours].

Proverbs 17:22: A happy heart is good medicine, and a joyful mind causes healing, But a broken spirit dries up the bones.

Philippians 4:8: Finally, believers, whatever is true, whatever is honorable and worthy of respect, whatever is right and confirmed by God's word, whatever is pure and wholesome, whatever is lovely and brings peace, whatever is admirable and of good repute; if there is any excellence, if there is anything worthy of praise, think continually on these things [center your mind on them, and implant them in your heart].

Proverbs 12:25: Anxiety in a man's heart weighs it down, But a good (encouraging) word makes it glad.

Deuteronomy 31:8: "It is the Lord who goes before you; He will be with you. He will not fail you or abandon you. Do not fear or be dismayed."

Ecclesiastes 9:4: [There is no exemption,] but whoever is joined with all the living, has hope; surely a live dog is better than a dead lion.

Psalm 9:9: The Lord also will be a refuge and a stronghold for the oppressed, A refuge in times of trouble;

Psalm 55:22: Cast your burden on the Lord [release it], and He will sustain and uphold you; He will never allow the righteous to be shaken (slip, fall, fail).

I Peter 5:7: casting all your cares [all your anxieties, all your worries, and all your concerns, once and for all] on Him, for He cares about you [with the deepest affection, and watches over you very carefully].

Helpful Resources

American Association of Christian Counselors
1-800-526-8673
www.aacc.net

SAMSHA's National Helpline
1-800-662-HELP(4357)
www.samhsa.gov
www.findtreatment.samhsa.gov

National Institute of Mental Health
1-866-615-6464
www.nimh.nih.gov

National Suicide Prevention Lifeline
1-800-273-8255
www.suicidepreventionlifeline.org

Mental Health America
1-800-273-TALK (8255)
www.mentalhealthamerica.net

Bibliography

American Psychiatric Association. (2013). *Diagnostic and statistical manual of mental disorders* (5th ed.). Arlington, VA: American Psychiatric Publishing.

CPSIA information can be obtained
at www.ICGtesting.com
Printed in the USA
FSHW011855030619
58565FS

Walking By Faith

Empowering Stories About Women Overcoming Depression

Rhonda and six courageous women share their personal journeys with depression in such a transparent way that readers are left able to identify the signs and symptoms of depression and take action to help themselves and others. She engages readers by exposing her vulnerabilities as a mental health professional who finds herself needing the very services that she provides as her livelihood. Rhonda charges the reader and the faith community to educate themselves about depression and other mental health disorders and become a part of the solution.

Rhonda Fuller Turner

$18.99
ISBN 978-0-9993256-3-6
51899>

9 780999 325636

A BIBLE STUDY BASED ON
AFRICAN AMERICAN SPIRITUALS

Plenty
Good
Room

AUDIO CD
ENCLOSED